REBECCA MILTON

How to Forgive Yourself in Fifteen Years

For Ben - I haven't given up just yet.

Contents

Foreword

Fifteen years ago, when I was at sixth form, I had a breakdown. I didn't know the words *depression* or *anxiety* when I was seventeen. I certainly didn't know the words *self harm* and I barely knew the word *suicide*. I learned them the hard way, trapped inside my own head, unable to escape their painful truth.

Poetry, for a long time, was the only way I could eject those thoughts safely. I don't remember starting to write poetry; as far as I'm aware, I always have. It was with me before I got sick, and is with me now, after the worst of those years. I hope that it will be with me forever.

This collection is that salvation. That verbalising of things that hurt too much to be spoken aloud. At times it does not pull the punches of that internal voice, so if you are triggered by discussion of self harm or suicide especially, please proceed with caution and care for your wellbeing.

I hope that nothing here resonates with you - but if it does, I hope it reminds you that you are not alone.

Phoenix

come with me into the forest
   where the shadows shall hide who we are;
   and our starlit dreams show the silvery gleams
   of our futures both near and so far.

let's reach up into that skyline.
   let's tear the impossible down.
   scream defiance at they who would stand in our way
   claim those dreams as our victory crown.

we don't have to settle for maybe
   we don't have to settle for could
   we don't have to be what they say we must be
   or worse still, succumb wholly to should.

and when we have won, we will leave here
   and we'll step right out into the light
   we will finally be seen as what we've always been
   even when we were shrouded in night.

and we'll walk through the world as the monarchs
   of all we have crushed 'neath our feet.

and we'll hold our heads high as we open the sky
to every scared dreamer we meet.

there are days

there are days when the world turns grey around her
   and pushes
     enfolding her in an embrace that has no touch
     until there is nothing left but the knot in her throat
     the weight in her gut
     the pressure behind her eyes that burns.
     there are days when she watches from above
     unable to reach the colours inside her;
     and there are days when she is nothing but feelings
     knotted up into a ball that she tries,
     futilely,
     to untangle from one another.
     there are days when she stands on the edge
     of a race
     coiled like a spring, ready to charge –
     longing to turn and streak across the marked lanes
     not caring where she runs
     so long as it is away, away from here, anywhere else.

Panic

The first sign is when everything gets louder.
  It's almost as if it all moved closer;
  the traffic noise is no longer peripheral,
  it's right there against her eardrums
  along with the chatter of people talking
  and the pulsing of her heartbeat –
  which is the second sign. Thumping faster,
  she's sure it's happening now.
  And she'll try, at length, to stop it –
  or at least to postpone the inevitable.

But this time it's too close, things are
  far too loud, wrapping her in a bubble.
  Then the tears, the part she hates the most,
  and not just because with it comes
  the tightening of her chest,
  the tense, thin-and-thick breaths too short
  to stem the tide of panic –
  because it's obvious now, everyone can see
  that she can't control herself
  can't stop her brain from running away with her.
  That's when her legs give out.

4

Her friends are clustered around her now,
   one's holding her hand
   the other has gone for water, as if it'll help.
   They don't know what to do,
   not any more than she does – but she tries,
   for them, to breathe. To breathe. Just
   to breathe.
   But it's too far now, her throat hitches,
   contracting in hysterical sobs about nothing.
   Nothing at all, and that's the worst part –
   because if there were a reason, she wouldn't
   mind this quite so much.

"I'm sorry," she garbles, over and over,
   as if there's any apology good enough
   to make up for the helplessness she's given them.
   This is when she starts to wonder
   if she's making it all up. Perhaps she's fine.
   Perhaps this is just an act, to get attention.
   The thought makes her sobs worse.
   She clutches her fingers against her throat,
   as if feeling the rapid beat of her heart
   will give her any more power to control it.

But slowly, she breathes. In and out.
   In and out. In and out. In and out.
   And slowly things get quieter.
   Her sobs die down to quiet shakes.
   She clings desperately to her friends,
   who against all odds haven't left her.
   And slowly, slowly, slowly she calms.

Shame wraps her in a cool blanket.
If only she were normal.

Achievement Hunter

When I am nestled at my desk
   with another game on the screen
   do not think of me as lazy.

Today I caught my hundredth pet
   and got the achievement for it,
   another star next to my name.

Do you think these things meaningless
   just because they're in pixels?
   Just because they're not real?

They're real to me, you know.
   And I don't mean I think a world
   where magic exists is real.

I mean that I really sat here
   for all the hours I have sat here
   and earned this golden star.

And maybe that's silly to you,
   but to me – to me, it's everything.

It's more than I thought I could do.

So please don't mock my hours
    spent grinding to max level,
    or collecting every beautiful thing.

Because this game, and all games,
    might just be the only thing
    reminding me that I'm still worthy.

anxiety

there is a kind of tiredness
   that aches itself through my bones
   a resonant song of fatigue
   that has nothing to do with my body.
   it is my mind's creation,
   this deep-seated exhaustion,
   and the only solution for it
   is to hide,
   hide,
   hide away
   where no one can find me –
   until I am ready
   to pretend myself confident
   all over again.

Impossible

I am so afraid
  of not knowing things
  and of being stupid

that I have this dream –
  a nightmare, really –
  that comes sometimes.

I've had it since
  I was young;
  I can't escape it.

It isn't a dream
  that's a story,
  more a feeling.

It's the idea that
  there's something
  impossible.

Impossible
  to understand;

to make sense of.

Like the feeling
    of forgetting a word
    trapped on your tongue,

but so strong
    it makes my heart
    clench into a fist.

So strong that
    I'm so afraid
    I wake up shaking –
    and that thing,
    that impossible thing,
    sits on me like lead.

It's in my mind;
    escaping it
    is so very hard.

And so I sit there
    small and stupid
    and so very afraid.

Because I can't
    explain I'm scared
    of something

so small and so
    stupidly simple

as not knowing.

Eye Contact

I never look people in the eyes.
   It isn't a deliberate choice; I just can't.
   I used to, once, when I was younger –
   when looking was less painful.
   Things made more sense then.
   You see, we look each other in the eyes
   to see emotions; opinions; thoughts
   made manifest in the lines of the face.

These days I have already decided
   what you think of me. What you feel.
   I never look you in the eyes, or anyone –
   I never give myself the chance to be wrong.
   So I keep my head and my eyes down
   and I walk through the world assuming
   that everyone thinks as little of me
   as I do of myself.

on this day

christmas time
  is when your pictures
  appear in
  my facebook feed

on this day! it proclaims.
  on this day
  you had not abandoned
  all of these people.

do you remember?
  they used to be friends,
  and you left
  saying nothing.

remember how terrible
  a person you were.
  we'll make sure
  you never forget.

Intrusive Thoughts

I like to think I can control my mind,
   but some things when imagined don't go right.
   I dream and cannot control my left arm;
   it doesn't lift, or turn – it just gets stuck.
   Sometimes if it's quite bad my leg goes too,
   and then my dream is ruined through and through.

Then some things happen when I am awake:
   I walk straight down the road, and in my mind
   my new phone falls – smashes against the path.
   And so I hold it tightly to my chest,
   or else get antsy that my pocket's doomed
   to fail because my clumsiness balloons.

Sometimes I'll walk quite smoothly down a street
   and all my mind will fill with just one thought –
   a vision of my ankles giving way,
   and sending me tumbling, askew and shamed.
   And soon each step I take is undermined;
   frustration the foundation of my mind.

And when I'm feeling my absolute worst,

because these thoughts have come to weigh me down,
I'll sit here by my desk and start to think
that I should bash my arm against its edge.
But worst of the worst things that fill my head
are all the ones that say, "You'll soon be dead."

Memory

I don't forget things;
    I just can't remember them.

The empty spot in my mind
    holds my heart
    and squeezes it dry,
    as if the blood could fill it.

I can look at a page
    I thought I'd never read
    and know for sure
    I've read it before.

But I don't remember it.

My mind has purged
    three years of my life
    and then some.

But it's not done.

It keeps stealing,

only giving back in pieces
that stab with sharp edges
into the gaps that remain.

I cannot remember
    why I cannot remember
    the things I remember.

Does that make sense?
    Does it make any sense at all?

scars

there are three lines
  on my right thigh
  which trace the depth
  of my pain.

they have healed now,
  turned to white
  slivers of what once
  gaped in red.

I do not look at them;
  it reminds me that
  there are worse scars
  on the inside.

the sort you don't see
  until you trip on
  a knot of feeling, grown
  to hide a hole.

I think I would rather
  have a hundred scars

that I could see than
one I couldn't –

but no. no. you see,
there is no scar
that can heal another
when it's made.

my depression's internal monologue

god
    what a small thing
    and you can't even do it right.
    I mean I'm not surprised
    you don't do anything right, really,
    or if you ever manage to it was probably
    someone else's success,
    and on the rare occasion
    that something goes wrong and it isn't your fault,
    it's just the world dealing justice
    for how fucking tedious you are.

honestly it's a wonder that
    anyone puts up with you – actually,
    maybe they shouldn't have to.
    you think you need help? no,
    you should just sit here, with me,
    because you are not worthy
    of any care they would give you
    and be sure
    that they'd be doing it because they are good
    and not because you are wanted.

your arm's on the desk
  lift it up and smash it down
  line your body with the bruises
  that you deserve.

it's all pointless anyway
  one day you are going to die
  and there will be nothing
  you will just not exist
  like when you are asleep
  there will be nothing
  nothingnothingnothingnothing -
  you want to know, don't you
  if it really is nothing at all
  maybe we could find out.

it's not like anyone would miss you.

because you're just not nice,
  if you're nice it's just an act,
  if you're acting it's not well,
  when you're well you're too loud and
  when you're sick you're a burden and
  no one wants to look at you
  because you are fat and ugly and
  no one wants to listen to your stupid smug voice
  you worthless little know it all
  who doesn't really know anything.

those scars on your thigh
  are not sufficient

to articulate how much of a waste of space
you truly are.

Raindrops

When I was twenty years old, I walked
   from my new dormitory in Borough to London Bridge
   all the way along the high street, at lunchtime,
   when the roads were teeming with buses
   and the pavements were full of people scrabbling for food
   before their precious hour of break was up.
   It was raining; not the sort of rain you can ignore
   but the sort where the raindrops are so large
   they sting your skin when they land upon it.

It seemed to bother the other people,
   who huddled under umbrellas that didn't help
   when the rain came sideways and ruined their suits.
   I didn't care. I didn't have an umbrella or even a coat,
   I was soaked from head to toe but really,
   that seemed irrelevant in comparison to everything else.

Because I was walking along the very edge of the path,
   the kerb itself, a thin strip of paler grey to border the dark,
   feeling the buses rush past me and stir the air.
   They couldn't have been going that fast, really;
   there was too much traffic for them to pick up pace.

And maybe that's the reason that I didn't act
on the thought that was in my head, resounding loud
every single time another bus passed me.

What if, it whispered, loud enough to drown out the rain
what if I took one step to the left – what then?
Sometimes I could feel the hitch in my breath,
the pulse of intent in my chest as I lifted my foot –
but it always went back down on the kerb,
propelling me onwards in the pouring rain
into the distance, far far away, where there was a better life.

And though sometimes my feet came to a halt
or sometimes I stumbled and had to be caught,
and though sometimes I still stand on kerbs and wonder,
I kept moving forward more than I went back
and I never went down the shortcuts to the side
and I am no longer standing on Borough High Street
drenched in the rain that seemed so insignificant
against the far bigger storm raging inside my head.

oblivion

you brush your teeth. change,
   gratefully, into your bedclothes.
   the dim light of your Kindle
   illuminates the room.

next to you, he's started snoring.
   you read to the sound, intermittent
   and infuriating, an hour passing
   without any effort at all.

then your eyes begin to close,
   and you place the book aside.
   sleep. you'll need it, up early,
   for once at least – you hope.

but one day…

no. not now. quick, imagine
   something. anything.
   you're Hermione Granger.
   you went back in time.

but one day you'll…

you're one of the Vanir,
    the Goddess of Thieves,
    here to steal the tesseract
    from Odin's deepest vaults.

but one day you'll die.

you can't destroy a thought
    except by replacing it, but
    you can't replace this one.
    it consumes you.

one day you are going to die.

push it out. get rid of it –
    you'll have to if you want
    any semblance of sleep.
    but it won't go. it won't budge.

one day you are going to die.

you want to scream.
    how do other people live
    knowing this truth?
    how does it not drown them?

one day you are going to die.

he's still snoring whilst

you struggle with the nature
of everything in the world
that you cannot control.

one day you are going to die.

trapped by the knowledge
that the sleep you crave
is a mirror of the oblivion
you fear.

one day you are going to die.

you reach for the fantasies;
they will not be enough
to free you.

like the tide

drag me out
   like the tide
   I know is
   coming for me

in time you
   will return me
   to the sand
   and firm ground

I know this
   now, after all
   the times we
   have danced these

steps that mean
   more than I
   can yet realise
   because I cannot

see the fact
   that each time

you drag me
a little less

that each time
my head goes
beneath the waves
a little less

that each time
the salt scours
my flailing body
a little less

and that each
time you pull
my mind away
I get stronger.

chasm

we are standing
    on identical mountains.
    there is a gulf of space between us –
    we try to jump, but mostly
    we just fall.

so instead
    we call out to each other.
    we talk across this space and then,
    it is not quite so wide
    as it was.

the words change us:
    we see that our mountains
    are the same – they're just far apart,
    different in space and time
    but somehow shared.

in the moment
    that we realise this
    the chasm shifts – no longer impossible.
    we jump with tears into

each other's arms.

then it returns.
   the gap opens its maw and
   pulls our mountains apart once more –
   we forget they are the same.
   but we'll remember.

isolation

shut everything out
   because some of it's bad
   and you'll never let in
   the things that are good.

the things that are good
   cannot come into your life
   until you open the door of
   your mind and your heart.

your mind and your heart
   are not really at war;
   they're just struggling
   to understand one another.

to understand one another
   we must be open and brave,
   vulnerable and scared as
   we climb into each other.

Words

When I forget
   the hundred thousand things
   I want to tell you
   or if I can't get the words
   into the conversation before
   it runs away from me,
   it feels like failure –
   like those hundred thousand things
   are slipping through my fingers
   and will never be real
   if I have not shared them with you
   which maybe is why, sometimes
   I talk just a little too much.

found

it took me so long
   to find you
   because you were there
   long before I stopped looking
   for the other half of my hope.

in that silence
   of hopelessness
   I heard the world laughing,
   for we were one
   and no one could imagine
   a world where we were apart.

you are clever, and ambitious,
   and careful and kind and creative,
   and in the hive of our mind
   you dare to disagree
   and make me better for it.

do not go far from me;
   I would not live in a world
   as silent as before the day

that I met you.

forwards, ultimately

straight lines aren't natural.
   remember that, when you take each step
   and worry that they're not quite one foot
   in front of the other. it isn't possible
   to keep on going without a little wobble
   here and there, now and then.
   you'll get to where you're going.
   you might get lost along the way,
   might wander off the path,
   might get distracted by things here and there but still
   you'll get there in the end.
   sometimes you need to look backwards
   to appreciate how far you've come.
   it's fine, so long as you never, ever
   stop looking forwards as you go one,
   two, one, two, an eternal march
   in a meandering line.

giving up

someone that I loved
  once told me –

(when everything hurt,
  and I did not know
  how to go on)

– that I should give up.
  that there was
  no point
  to anything.

I was brave enough
  to ignore them.

years later, my brother
  gave me a gift.
  a hunk of marble.
  it said:

"never, ever, ever
  give up"

so I haven't.

Acknowledgements

I once wrote a story at high school about the experience of being bullied. My English teacher quietly gave it an A5 - our highest mark - and wrote, in red pen, "it's said that writing is revenge upon the world - I think you've just taken it". This wasn't the first time that someone had told me to write, but it's one that's stuck with me. I wouldn't be here without encouragement like that.

My high school music teacher, on the other hand - who was my favourite teacher - also wrote that I was "an excellent student who would be exceptional if she learned to ask for help". Good news! I did. Eventually.

So thank you first of all to my incredible partner, who has been with me for ten of these fifteen years now. Who loved me as much when I couldn't get out of bed as he does now that I'm healthy enough to tell him to clean the damn bathroom.

Thank you to my editor, Jo, who on top of being a magical word genius, accidentally became the best friend I'd always wanted. Thank you to my little big brothers and my incredible mother; I wish you understood less of this book, but I'm grateful for how much we understand each other now. Thank you to my second family, who have made me feel part of their incredible team since day one, and never judged me for struggling.

But most of all, more than anything, thank you to my doctors. My psychiatrists. My therapists. Every single person whose knowledge and skill has helped me to get to this point.

Without you, I would never have even started to forgive myself.